Meaningless Platter Dudes

Language Transformed on a Platter of Fun

Meaningless Platter Dudes

Language Transformed on a Platter of Fun

CAROLYN BISHOP

IGUANA

Copyright © Carolyn Bishop, 2012
Published by Iguana Books
460 Richmond St. West, Suite 401
Toronto, Ontario, Canada
M5V 1Y1

Editor: Lisa Sparks
Book layout design: Greg Ioannou and Stephanie Martin
Cover design: Jane Goodwin
Author photo: Kim Anderson

Library and Archives Canada Cataloguing in Publication

Bishop, Carolyn, 1949-
    Meaningless platter dudes: language transformed on a platter of fun /
Carolyn Bishop.

Also issued in electronic formats.
ISBN 978-1-927403-17-4

    1. English language—Humor. I. Title.

PN6231.W64B58 2012   428.102'07   C2012-905557-3

This is the original print edition of *Meaningless Platter Dudes*.

This book is dedicated to Art Clifford, who dislikes most puns yet spurred me on by saying, "That's just awful!"

Many thanks to the talented Iguana crew for their collective wisdom and sound guidance.

Herein are things I wake up thinking. A few might be considered unsuitable for children, because that's the kind of thing I wake up thinking.

"If we couldn't laugh, we would all go insane."
– Jimmy Buffet

THE GREAT OUTDOORS

A baby ate my dingo.

Don't fool with Nother Mature.

Shouldn't you be out walking your dogma?

The way to a shrub-lover's heart is through his sumac.

Heavy snowfall after mid-March is Mother Nature's way of telling you she's not really your mother.

Carolyn Bishop

Oh, how I miss those endless summe...

I'm afraid of October until the falling leaves.

Because only French underwear would do, Meredith bought zebras.

A bird in the hand is worth the price of tiny bird diapers.

If you don't like seabirds, albatross with you.

Out of seaweed? Relax! Kelp is on the way.

OCCUPATIONAL HAZARDS

Too many deadlines? Cover them with cosmetics.

To Beatles-loving bureaucrats, happiness is a form done.

Though in perfect health, Denton spent all his free time in hospital triage so he could become a good waiter.

When your troops yell "Ambush!" don't retort with "Are not!"

Carolyn Bishop

The optimistic teacher always sees the class as half full.

The funerals of respected newscasters are always attended by a broad cast of mourners.

Though attacked for her work, Margaret Mead never felt the need to anthropologize.

My intrusively talkative nature was an asset in my job as a United Nations interrupter.

I thought all I'd need to be an innkeeper was two wrists.

Scrooge's butler never maid enough to chauffeur his efforts.

Seafarers, beware! No wind fills your sails in the Straits of Jib Falter.

Semi-retired veterinarians still work in their spayer time.

Should I become incapacitated, I hereby appoint my ambulance driver as power of a gurney.

There was a time when a ghostly lady in an orchestra was treated like a band she.

They won't let me be a crossing guide because I'm not a curb scout.

Overcrowded with UN delegates, the elevator became a plummet meeting.

I think I sew too much. I sense a pattern.

On Clyde's birthday, his orthodontist wished him many gappy returns.

Oily riser Derek knew the drill.

It's not cheap to become a kickline dancer in New York. I had to buy my own Rockette launcher.

Locking myself in at my workshop was a problem. I was caught between the bevel and the cheap blue key.

There's nothing stuffier than a cab full of taxidermists.

Passive pencils are so easily lead.

If you need help replenishing inventory, hire a dedicated stalker.

7

If you lady magicians get wet paint on your underwear, a bra could dab ya.

Bogus philatelist seeks stamp of authenticity.

Brace yourself for discount dentistry.

Creditors are odd ducks. They bill you!

Good teachers seat students randomly. Otherwise the class is always keener on the other side.

Good waiters don't point toward the restroom when you ask for Dijon.

Forensic science students have a better chance of getting in on the found gore.

Derek's bulimia makes him special. He's the only Yankees shortstop to become a binge Jeter.

Dennis finally realized it would be less painful to bang his wall against a brick head.

Ham actors can't be cured.

9

Carolyn Bishop

On their birthdays, do shoe
fetishists blow out all their
sandals?

Harbingers are dangerously
addicted to laughter.

ENTHUSIASM

Laziness is its own reward.

Less Sarah Palin and more
serotonin, please.

I'd like to be respectful instead of
acquiescent, but I can't tell the
deference.

I don't think I'm unoriginal, and
I'm sure I'm trite about that.

I love your horn of plenty, but
how corn you cope, Pia?

Carolyn Bishop

I always see the most exciting games from the best seats in the Hyperbole!

I could have designed a great observatory if I'd known how to plan a tarium.

ALIENATION

Suddenly unintuitive, Quasimodo wants his hunch back.

The physics awards ceremony host has stage fright. He = mc scared.

The old block just isn't the same without Chip.

Penny had misgivings about being traded for thoughts.

I didn't like Star Trek. It shatnered my illusions.

Mason found every experience jarring.

Poor Gerald just found out his catty shopaholic girlfriend is a mall tease.

Not prone to nostalgia, the only thing Lou consistently missed was the point.

I'm so socially insecure that I once stuffed myself into the Cuisinart just so I could blend in.

I'm told my ignorance gives me a certain je ne sais quoi.

In the early 20th century, my grandfathers were always getting into spats.

If you think earthlings are stuck in their ways, you should see the folks inErtia Major!

I regret wearing shoes last night. They made me feel so shoddy.

If Ayn Rand had been more pleasant, she might have been at last hugged.

Nothing cripples book sales like hack-kneed prose.

15

Carolyn Bishop

Professors shouldn't have to explain to students that Norman Mailer wasn't a French letter.

I'm suddenly afraid of my car. It's become peugeotlistic.

Hoping to cure his profound listlessness, Henry acquired a New York telephone directory.

It's not that I'm evil. I just need more exorcize.

I suck at meeting new people. I always ask, "How do I do what?"

LAW AND ORDER

It won't help you to break out in hives. Those bee disguises don't fool the prison guards.

Nothing goes better with an x-rated crime movie than a big bowl of cop porn.

The RCMP are on horseback so much that it's no wonder they have Musical Rhoids.

Police have charged an Aldershot man with arborcide.

Police verified that mint sauce was on the lamb.

A police spokesman couldn't say off the top of his head why the victim had been decapitated.

No one knows why Elmer turned pasty and died. Police seek more glues.

Dear Illuminati Customer Service: Please expedite my New World Order.

I wove through traffic until police confiscated my loom.

I knew I was defenceless at the salad bar when I salmagundi.

ANIMAL CRACKERS

When Mickey's daffy mouse bugs goofy bunnies, Donald ducks.

Zoos are often worse places than they look. Don't let the pen grins fool you.

When I offered to walk her dog, Suzette thought I was pulling her chien.

The tardy worm avoids the early bird.

Rocking horses tend to be apple losers.

Wearing tight snakeskin clothing is just asking for a hissy fit.

Simon and Garfunkel climate change threatens the fridge over troubled otters.

Sit down, kitty. I have something to tell you about your parents, and I can't cougar-coat it.

Omar's pachyderm is so huge it makes Allah faint.

A cat, a pat; a purr, what fur!

"The Walrus and the Carpeter" appeals to rug rats, whereas culinary students enjoy the entire *Through the Cooking Class.*

Some said Porky Pig was ugly, but I thought he was especially hamstrung.

Marsupials are fond of pouched eggs as long as they aren't koalagulated.

The endangered animal named after the adventurous Greek god of love is the whynoteros.

My pampered cat has lined knives.

My puppy Ko-Ko is a nanki-poodle dandy.

Dress well for meals, but don't dine with your capon.

He'd been in a stupor for daze, so I gave my catatonic.

I'd take my boxer to church if he weren't so pewgilistic.

23

Easy varks make better pets than aard ones do.

Are mole asses really that slow in January?

If you llama take you on a picnic, alpaca the lunch.

Last night my poodle went to a buffet with the girls. They all whelped themselves.

It gets my goat when people butt in without considering the ramifications.

My cat will go crazy in Germany, but I'll feed her sane.

I shouldn't have named my horse Ralph Lauren. Now he feels polorized.

Diners who ordered the lemming chiffon pie left the restaurant in droves.

It scares the pants off people when my cat Jodh purrs.

DOES TRAVEL BUILD CHARACTER?

I must get a closer look at Norway. I've never scanned a navia.

To avoid Capricorns, wear comfy shoes at Italian resorts.

Be a suiteheart and book me a heated room at the RadIsOn.

Down underwear is Tad's mania.

No, congenial Canada's motto is not "a merry tusk admired."

When visiting Toronto, you can scour borough bluffs, but please don't tip the dawn valet.

The rain in Spain can damn well stay there.

On hearing "A band on ship!" delighted *Titanic* passengers flocked to the ballroom.

Fly Boozy Airlines. We don't count our check-ins before they're smashed.

27

Francis Drake couldn't wait for the yellow paint on his chamber pot to dry. Hence the Golden Hind.

If your luggage is stolen in Port Manteau, just call the valise.

My neighbours want me to tear down my island home. To them it's an Azore.

My yacht *Typeface* has hit a serif.

Wistful armchair travellers, rejoice! A cent a mental journey is a really good deal!

You can always identify the linguists at the beach by their diphthongs.

Horton hears a hooligan.

Mickey Mouse animation bugs bunnies.

Some kids want a trip to South America for Christmas. That's where the Christ of the Candies is.

I'd have a much broader education if I hadn't been sent to a miniscule.

Carolyn Bishop

Divorced women used to give up garter belts for the snake of the children.

I just flotilla my ship comes in.

FAMILY TIES

Laura wants to explain the consequences of procrastination to her son, but she keeps putting it off.

My homicidal great-grandmother wore stays of execution.

My family moves around so mysteriously that I can't telekinesis from the kinephews.

Did Dadaists celebrate Father's Day?

I really don't think police should tell voyeurs to peep it in the family.

I suspect my somnolent aunt might be a napkin.

Long after a bitter divorce, the Flashertons are still accusing each other of indecent ex-spousesure.

Why am I so peacefully domestic? Amnesty, I guess.

AMBIVALENCE

Though some called him lazy and others called him cowardly, Sitwell held to his firm belief that no sacrifice is too small to reconsider.

CINEMA FAIT RIEN

It's ironic that Frances was pretty much the only sober one on the set of *A Coppola Sips Now.*

Though originally reluctant to ingest an entire hen, Russell Crowe was Gladiator.

There's poor plumbing in the land of Oz, so some swear over the drain flow.

The last time I waltzed, it made me feel Disney.

NAME THAT TUNE

Cyndi's hairstyle kept getting shorter because she's a Lauper, and curls just want to have fun.

We're ardent lepers' only arts club band.

Remember the good old days when white rabbits flew free on the Jefferson Air Plan?

The three stages of some folk singers' relationships are peter, pall, and marry.

When gardeners are sunny and share, the beets grow on.

Don't it always seem to go that you don't know what you've got 'til it's pawned?

When it comes to e-readers, R&B musicians know KoBo Diddley squat.

For frustrated golfers, the cursed putt is the bleepest.

My musical kettle is always spouting flat études.

Carolyn Bishop

While in tractor transit, commemorative Hendrix timepieces are all along the watch tower.

Ostentatious stalker Elgar took the pomp and lurk 'em stance.

When the canvas falls on ZZ Top, everybody's crazy 'bout a tarp-pressed band.

Carole King's little workshop has been shut down. Its tool ate Baby.

LET'S GET THIS STRAIGHT

Yo, neighbour with thin walls!
When you be jammin', Ibuprofen.

I thought I heard a woman's
voice, but it was just a guise.

Why do the noisiest weddings
have the fewest hushers?

I have optional convictions, so
you're lucky this isn't a lifelong
sentence.

Carolyn Bishop

How did Nobel hear his phone ring?

NEOLOGISTICS

A peerage is not incontinence-related anger.

Saggy butt? You need a lowbottomy.

You may call me a sailor; but I'm a nice girl, so don't call me ahoy.

Why complain occasionally when you could be doing it habitchually?

You went to your a.m. hula class, undulate for work.

By happy accident, Jess invented the immersible cling-wrap Sarandipity.

When I attended Icarus's funeral he'd been daedalus than a few days.

WRITE IT OFF

The release date of *The Pit and the Pendulum* was Poe timing.

We uptight grammarians don't fear death. It's the only way to get past tense.

When Hamlet sets himself on fire, his hose and pants and silken stern are red.

Et tu, blue tush?
#coldthronemisquotes

Carolyn Bishop

Helvetica is the font of all
Swissdom.

The job I vonnegut is at
Slaughterhouse-Five.

Louisa may be a little woman, but
she's all caught up.

I'm puzzled by cryptic comments
made in cross words.

It feels like sentries since I started
guarding my words.

Hire an editor. You need
that/which hunter.

44

When it comes to omissions, I have no elisions.

As a tribute to sad birds, Bram wrote *The Legend of Weepy Swallow.*

After I plagiarized lines from "The Raven," I was relieved to be told it was après-Poe.

His boasts about his high tolerance for soaking up alcohol were just a sop's fables.

I heard J. D. Salinger ordered his assistant to put a hold on field calls.

45

Carolyn Bishop

My little horse enjoys every fairy
tale except *Little Red Gelding Rod*.

I don't let my kids read *Hamlet*
because of the ho ratio.

Dodi claims she could have
written Dr. Zhivago herself if it
hadn't been past her knack.

For fringe-group poetry, nothing
beats TV's *Sects and the Ditty*.

Like Romeo, you can't
surmontague nightmares by
sweeping them under the capulet.

Iphigenia's in Tarsus, then what's in the bottle?

A PRACTICAL SOLUTION

Ending the stench of ill-considered wars might be easier if septic tanks were deployed.

WHAT'S IN A NAME?

Alice is happy with her name, but
Aloysius to change his.

Vladimir is glad I'm here.

I go out all the time, but
Anastasia's home.

If some idiot uses your assumed
name, pseudonymrod.

Must you always put everything
down, Plunkett?

Carolyn Bishop

Samurai, but who are you?

FOOD FOR THOUGHT

My name is Malibu Bob, and I'll be your surfer tonight.

All Herb wanted was to have just one more good thyme before he dried.

You can eat all the pie and ice cream you want, but it won't change the fact that you've been desserted.

Too young to remember Sam &
Dave, Kyle assumes it was a fish
entree.

When you chart your weight loss,
s'at your rated fat? Weary of
Mulligan's self-inflicted problems,
friends let him stew in his own
juice.

Return stale cake to the baker, and
don't accept his frosty retortes.

The processed-meat aisle made
Casey as excited as a can in a
kidney store.

My Springsteen-themed chili restaurant "Born to Run" was doomed from the start.

The singing waiter tried to warn me with "Won't You Be My Vermincelli Baby?"

My nitrogenous chicken Alka loid an egg!

My only complaint about the channel crossing was the left-Dover food.

Miller's always the first to get in on the ground flour.

My halo is too big for my hat. It's a well-fed aura.

Higgins agreed that royal weddings should be as spectacular as the indigestible cakes made in their honour.

I haven't had minced seafood since I was knee-high to a bass chopper.

Some people make preserves just because they can.

Eat oranges and attain piece of rind.

Does the cord on bleu chef make him sad and unproductive?

If you want a sparse diet, eat lots of paltry.

I took a cheesy online tech course and became a certified feta processor.

Because they were men after her own heart, Anna had a thing for cannibals.

I tried to make beef jerky from a rump roast, but it just sat there on its ass.

Carolyn Bishop

Chef Henri's technique with eggs was irrepoachable.

Learn gourmet fish cookery and make the world a better plaice.

GRAPE EXPECTATIONS

Amelia discovered too late how hard it was to travel light with a suitcase full of Chianti.

For inmates in upscale prisons, wine with meals is cause for cell libation.

He criticized my homemade wine, so I let him have it with both barrels.

My sister stopped speaking to me just because I gave her kid a Dr. Soused book.

Barry Jr. never knew how vexing aging could be until he indulged in elder Barry whine.

Tea totallers always count the bags under your eyes.

I think my bank account has a drinking problem. It can't keep its balance.

SELL IT TO ME

Frustrated Blackberry investors
remain dead RIM believers
#knowyourMonkees

I don't trust textile manufacturers.
They're all fabricators.

We need devices to compensate
for de virtues.

Remember, at Michelangelo
Inferior Facelifts you get the
agony without the elasticity.

MAYHEM

Design flaws and an oblivious captain cause "unsinkable" Facebook to strike a zuckerberg.

The amount of online work to be done is in direct proportion to the crappiness of the internet connection.

The ancient computer found under a fragrant bush surely verifies the story of *Samsung and de Lilac*.

France blows tech edge, kills
Marie Internet, and Robespierre to
PayPal.

If you love a parade, pick a spot
online and watch the false beliefs
march past.

WE HAVE A PROBLEM

Dusty felt as if he were living in a vacuum.

I'm no good at going out on dates. I keep falling off.

My ancient math teacher flunked me, abacus I broke out in a beady sweat.

Selfish Sammy clings to his firm belief that no sacrifice is too small to reconsider.

I might stop all my needleless swearing and just take up darning.

I'm having the worst luck sending mail by lamppost.

DISGRUNTLED?

Avery grew to resent the constant labelling.

Face bandaged and in great pain, Arnold began to doubt the efficacy of keeping his nose to the grindstone.

MISSED OPPORTUNITIES

To be just insipid enough to succeed requires bland ambition.

I'd never felt truly thanked in France until I heard Marci's beau coo.

If at first you don't succeed, try another cliché.

They won't let you on that plane to Florida if you say, "My, I'm a bitch."

No handyman, Diego couldn't salvador even if his life hinged on it.

No matter how fast and flexible I am, I just can't do the rush limbo.

No one warned Bert that sidewalk maintenance work could be so pedestrian.

If Paul Simon were a rapper, he'd still be Jay-Z after all these years.

Darla failed her music exam because she thought harpsichord was Laura's brother.

I flunked Philosophy 101 because during lectures I read elitist comics. Most of them were aristofunnies.

Having lost everything at the track, Al tells himself that's just the way the bookie bumbles.

WEAR AND TEAR

It's Kelly's own fault that her son wears her clothes. She keeps skirting the issue.

When a rusty tap won't turn on, Brooklyn natives try to faucet.

My roofing expenses are killing me soffitly.

FAILURE TO COMMUNICATE

Because of one little typo, Jim lost his bid to build a better mousecrap.

Hammerstein never learned why he was banned from his favourite pub.

INSPIRATIONAL THOUGHTS

Cheer up, Spaniards! It's always marquess before the don.

This cretin is the better part of pallor.

JUST PLAIN RUDE

As Jiminy Cricket aged, did it take
him longer to zippa de doodad?

Dave supposed a Peter Pan was as
good as any other place to store it.

Does the flat you lent your tutor
still smell bad?

Last time Dennis showed some
spunk, his teacher made him put
his pants on and go home.

SEX AND THE WITTY

Dana's considerate kinky beau always called when he was tied up at the office.

Ed hasn't looked forward to Victoria Day since he found out she isn't a stripper.

I wonder how many former fashion models get arrested as indecent ex-posers.

Lulu's affair with her phone stalker made her hot under the caller.

HOLIDAY MAGIC

To frustrated December anglers, it's beginning to look a lot like missed bass.

I have only one decoration this year, and it's rude. All I want for Christmas is my too-blunt wreath.

To celebrate the joy of Isthmus, all I want is a straitforward set of Archipe Lego.

Merry Christmas, grammarians! Don't make the presents tense.

I like Boxing Day meals, but they take forever to eat with those big padded gloves.

Last Halloween I made the mistake of demanding trick or gnosis.

SCREENPLAY

If you need a playground, just shred the script.

THE WHEELS OF COMMERCE

At Fake Diamonds we put our solder to the rhinestone.

Wallet monetize your speech to purse your lips?

Welcome to RetailGiant, where we train our cashiers to be courteous to everyone except you.

The first sign that you've lost your factory job is sudden shiftlessness.

Tread carefully in furniture stores. There are stools everywhere.

TYLENOL® makes me hallucinate. I see the men of fins.

Viking currency was easy to come by because it stuck out like a Thor sum.

At Slightly Friendly Appliances we greet you with a microwave.

It's not so much fun for kids at Can Tank "R" Us.

When Botox, lips listen.

Said the big oil company to its critics, "Who you callin' an Esso?"

It's too bad about the wee typo in the ad for "Acne Fine Cosmetics."

I've invented an attractive litter box for stupid cats. I call it the Bincomepoop™

AFTERMATH

When the rivers dry up, people
will ask, "Where have all the
flowers gone?"
#peterpaul&maryfuture

Bin Laden bin hadden.

The debates in our kitchens aren't
the same without Hitchens.

Too much sun has made me sore
and tancankerous.

When Marty pled guilty and went
to prison, he felt all fessed up with
no place to go.

HOLLY WOULD

A good editor would have changed the horror-film title to *The Curse of the Waswolf.*

Don't believe Hollywood gossip. Susan Saran don has nothing to do with the cling-wrap mafia.

I liked the emptiness of *2001: a Space Odyssey* as I walked along its hollowed Hals.

MUSICAL CHAIRS

Audiophiles see the whirled
through Bose-coloured glasses.

He claims to sing well in
washrooms, but he just lips sinks.

Oh give me a home where the
buff also roam.

As the best-dressed but most
boring American actor in *The
Mikado*, I'm a Nanky-Poo dull
dandy.

Carolyn Bishop

Hey, Mr. tanned marine man,
display a thong for me.

My '70s rock concert experience
became a Marx Brothers farce
when they led Zeppo in.

It's 50 years since the Rolling
Stones began falling on their own
Jagger.

No, you are not the Walrus.

CAUSE FOR OPTIMISM

The upside of nothing else coming to mind is that nothing else has to make room for it.

CONFLICT OF INTEREST

Hospital demolition was blocked by the outspoken townsfolk, who never minced wards.

Watering my gardens by hand was too aggravating this year. Next year I'm digging an irritation canal.

I was all for intelligent transportation until I boarded a thinking ship.

If a knife-wielder threatens you,
just mention your instability.

Gift shopping makes me so tense
that in future I'll walk right past
perfect presents.

BRUSH WITH FAME

Last night I dreamed there was a prize for making an emergency phone call, and mine won one!

The prize I won for my new head restraint was a tether in my cap.

Do I win atrophy for my tight jeans?

TECHNOBRAINER

Ats! Thee's no on my keyboad!

I have a theory about data, but I can't back it up.

For superfluous information, visit furthermoreandplusredundant.com.

LEARNING CURVE

Can swearing be retracted?
Discuss.

IT MAKES THE WORLD GO ROUND

Distraught on a bridge over love gone sour, Beau cried out, "Why cantilever?"

Tonight I'm breaking up with my usher boyfriend. We can't go on seating like this.

I was touched by my nephew's pet spider's dying words: "Tarantula I love her."

GOD ONLY KNOWS

Dear Bible,

Why do your scary parts have to be part of the deal?

Yo, God! What's with advising a 600-year-old man in a comparably corrupt society to build a getaway ark but telling us diddly-squat?

At the gospel-based furniture outlet, a swing-low suite chair I bought.

When Dylan hears knock, knock, knockin' on heaven's door, he don't think twice. It's Saul Wright.

I finally dusted my bookcase when I remembered that God helps those who help themshelves.

If your child is waiting for the Rapture, it's ascension-seeking behaviour.

I'll never be a saint. I don't have the right beatitude.

I'm practising Japanese mysticism but can't sigh an aura yet.

93

Carolyn Bishop

My spiritual life began at Shirley
Temple.

If only people worshipped me.
Then I could retire and get
reverence pay.

For the Record

Some recording execs in the digital age are female, but most are just meaningless platter dudes.

Iguana Books

iguanabooks.com

If you enjoyed *Meaningless Platter Dudes*...

What can we say? There's nothing else like it. Buy lots of copies so Carolyn is inspired to write more.

iguanabooks.com/blog/

You can also learn more about Carolyn Bishop and her upcoming work on her blog.

carolynbishop.iguanabooks.com/blog/

If you're a writer...

Iguana Books is always looking for great new writers, in every genre. We produce primarily ebooks but, as you can see, we do the occasional print book as well. Visit us at iguanabooks.com to see what Iguana Books has to offer both emerging and established authors.

iguanabooks.com/publishing-with-iguana/

If you're looking for another good book...

All Iguana Books books are available on our website. We pride ourselves on making sure that every Iguana book is a great read.

iguanabooks.com/bookstore/

Visit our bookstore today and support your favourite author.

IGUANA

www.ingramcontent.com/pod-product-compliance
Lightning Source LLC
Chambersburg PA
CBHW072043040426
42447CB00012BB/2994